Table of Cont

HOW TO READ EXERCISES.

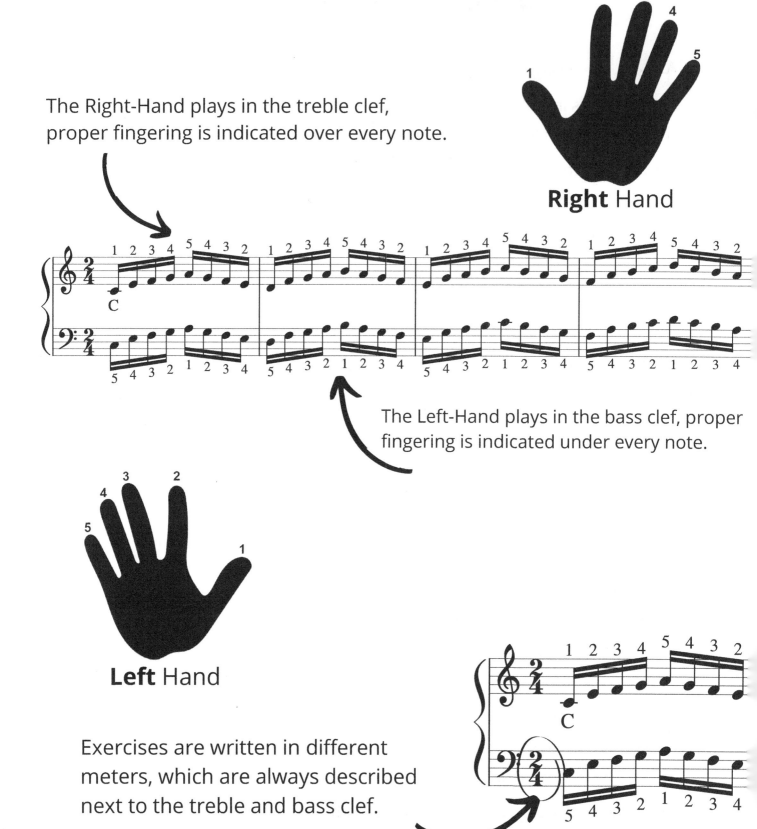

The Right-Hand plays in the treble clef, proper fingering is indicated over every note.

Right Hand

The Left-Hand plays in the bass clef, proper fingering is indicated under every note.

Left Hand

Exercises are written in different meters, which are always described next to the treble and bass clef.

1

NOTE NAMES IN BOTH CLEFS.

Treble Clef

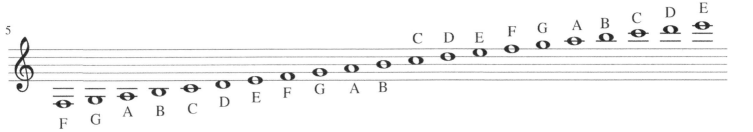

Bass Clef

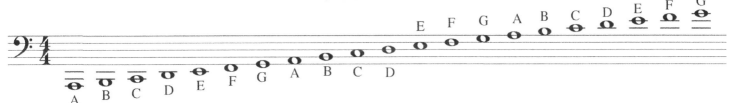

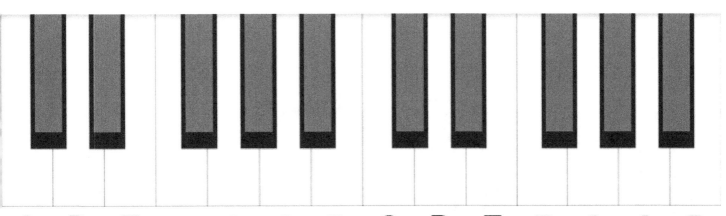

PIANO KEYS MARKING.

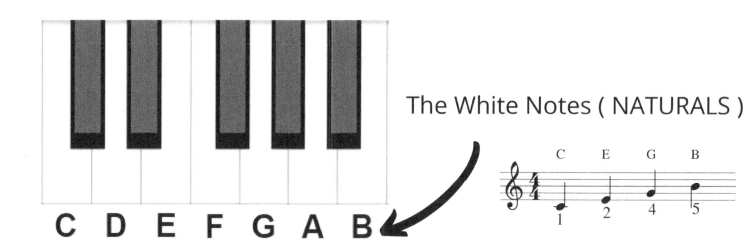

C D E F G A B

The White Notes (NATURALS)

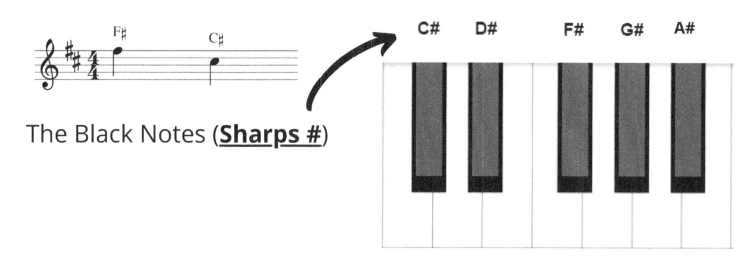

The Black Notes (**Sharps #**)

C# D# F# G# A#

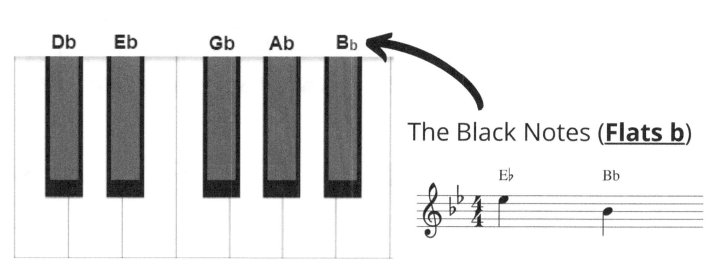

Db Eb Gb Ab Bb

The Black Notes (**Flats b**)

CIRCLE OF FIFTHS.

Circle of Fifths and Fourths

The circle of fifths and circle of fourths are musical tools used to explore the relationships between key signatures.

The circle of fifths is a graphical representation of all key signatures with sharps and flats. The notes are arranged in a circle in such a way that each note is connected to another note a perfect fifth away when moving clockwise, or a perfect fourth away when moving counterclockwise.

The circle of fifths enables musicians to easily discover the connections between notes in a specific key signature, making composition, improvisation, and chord progression creation easier.

Both circles are valuable in the composition and improvisation process as they help musicians understand which notes fit within a particular key signature and which do not. The circle of fifths is particularly intriguing because it reveals the cyclical nature of the relationships between key signatures. For instance, when moving along the circle of fifths, we can observe that each subsequent key signature differs by one sharp or flat, which affects the sound and character of a composition. Thus, the circle of fifths serves not only as a practical tool but also as an inspiring source for musicians seeking new combinations of sounds and harmonic colors.

The diagram below represents major and minor key signatures with sharps and flats.

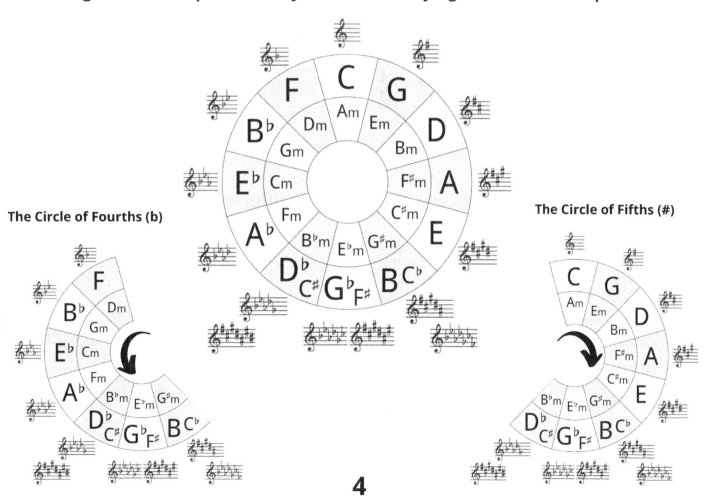

The Circle of Fourths (b)

The Circle of Fifths (#)

HOW TO UNDERSTAND AND READ "KEYS"

In keys, there is a sharp symbol (#) and a flat symbol (b)
Sharp (#) up the note by a semitone and flats (b) down by a semitone.

Example:

Sharp **(#)** is on the fifth line, because of that the **F** sound
is upgraded to **F#**, the same with the **C -> C#.**

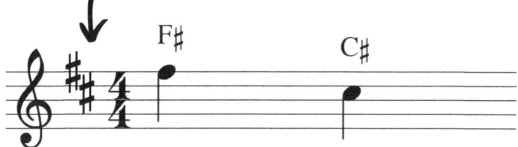

Flats **(b)** lies in the fourth field, so the sound **E** is
lowered to **Eb**, just like **B -> Bb**

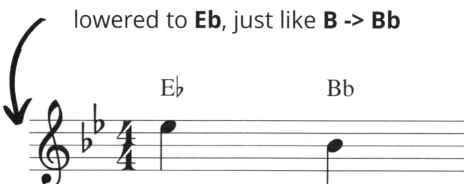

The more sharps or flats in the key signature, the more we play the black keys.

The exercises are written in **12** different keys.

Sharp Keys "#":
C Major (0)
G Major (1)
D Major (2)
A Major (3)
E Major (4)
B Major (5)
F# Major (6)
C# Major (7)

Flat Keys "b":
F Major (1)
Bb Major (2)
Eb Major (3)
Ab Major (4)

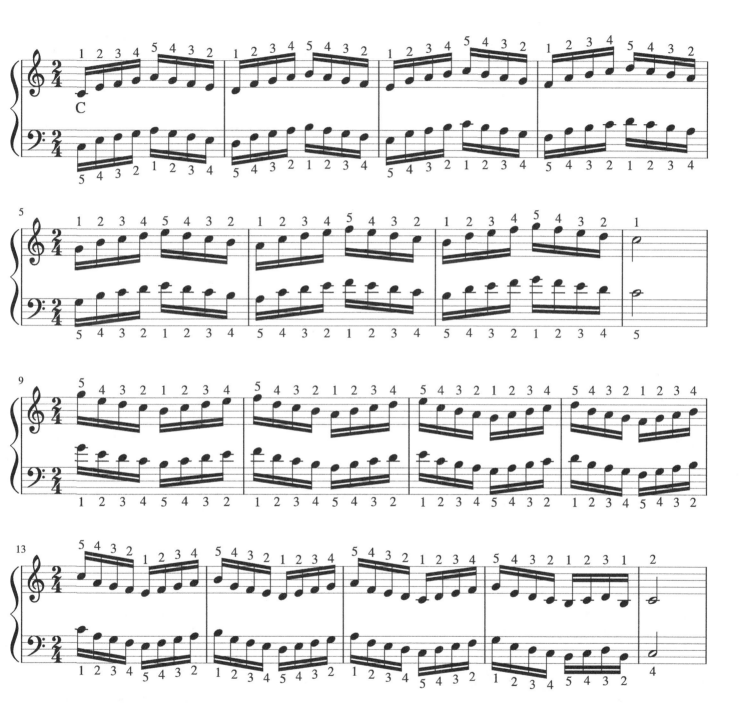

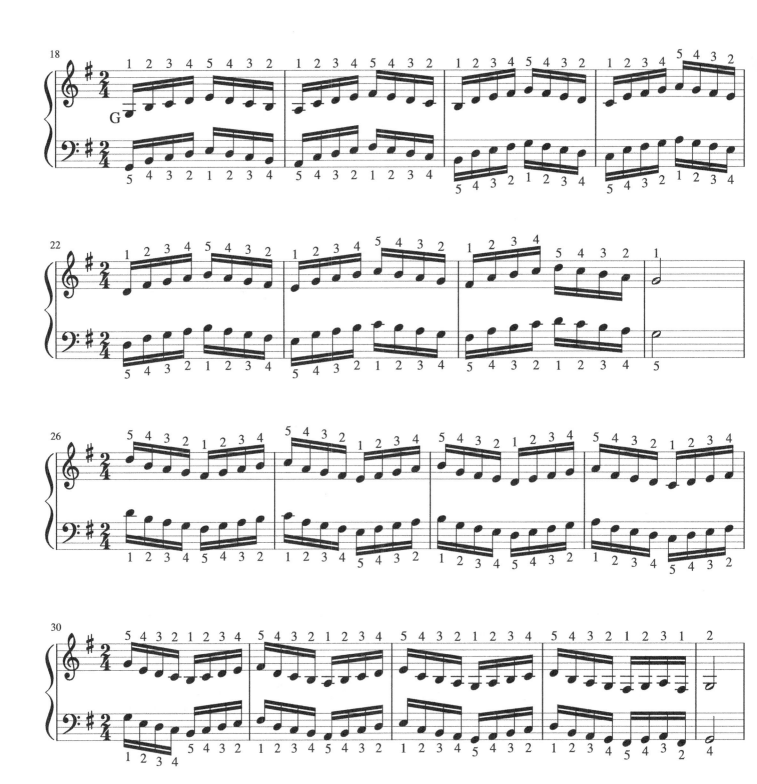

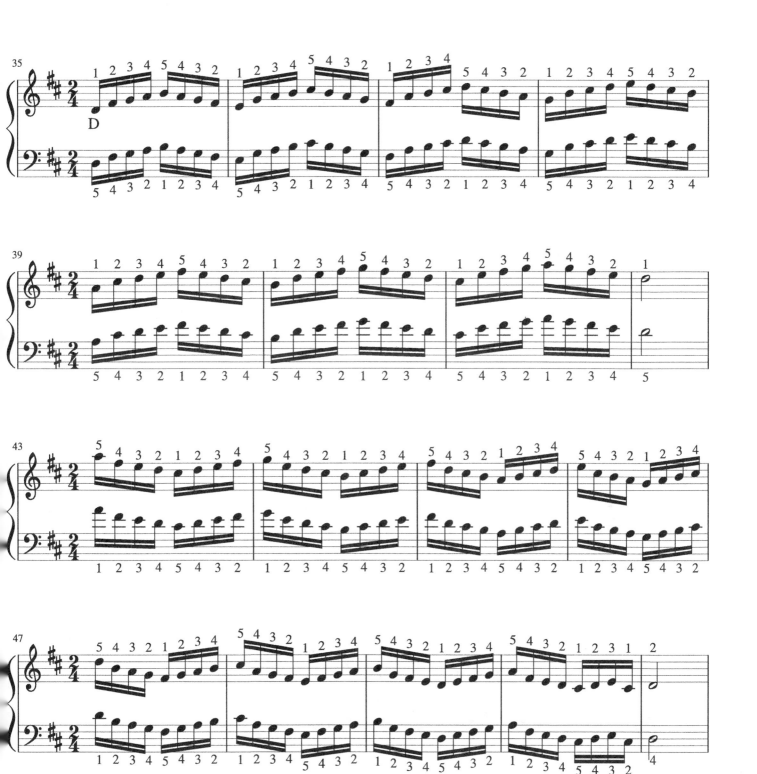

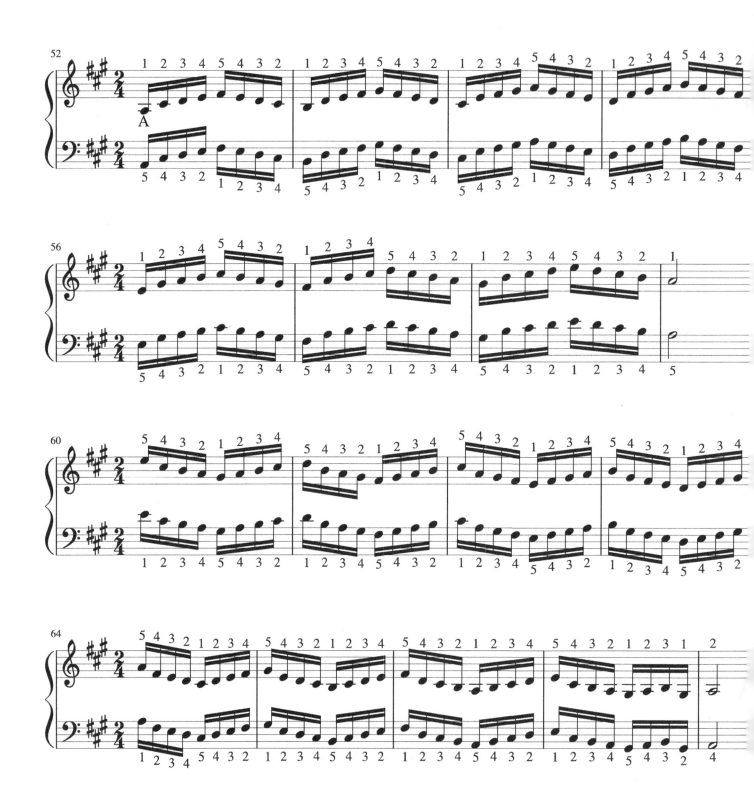

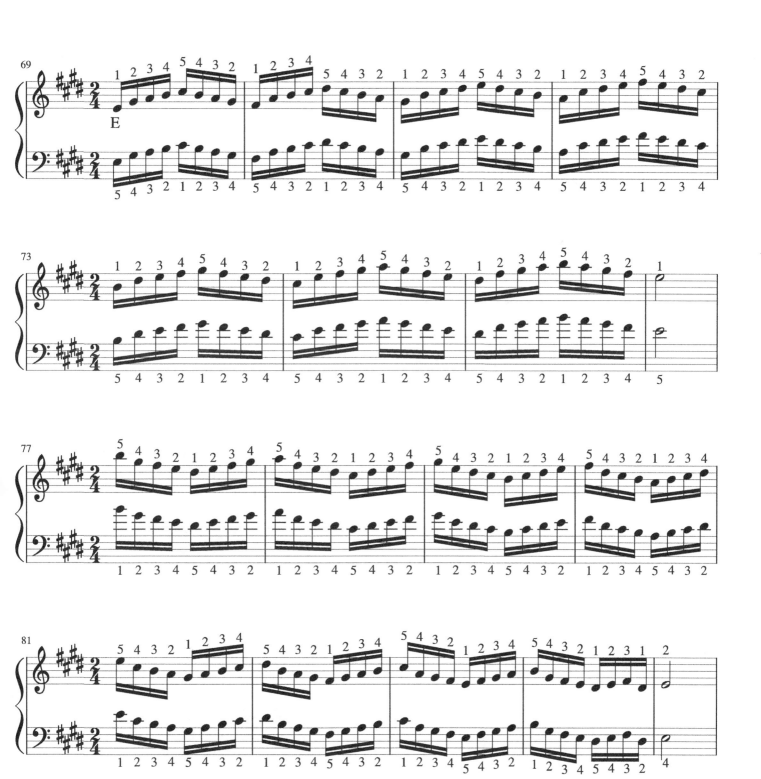

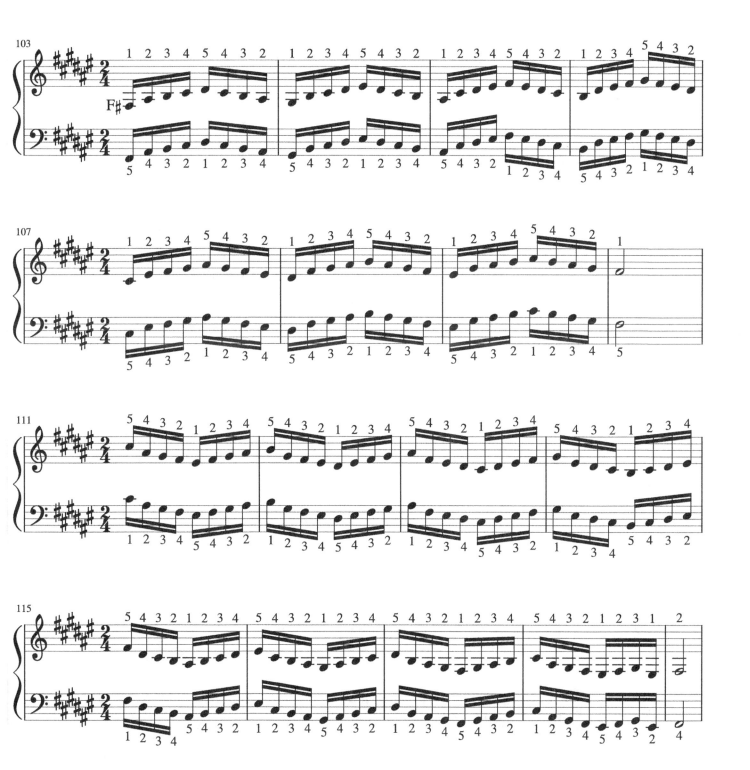

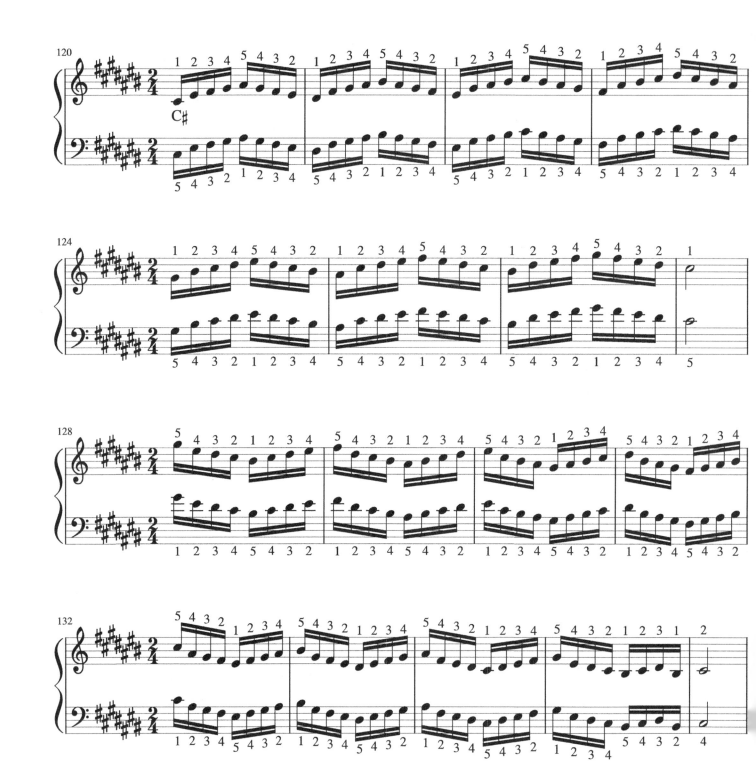

EXERCISES FOR BOTH HANDS IN F MAJOR Vol 1

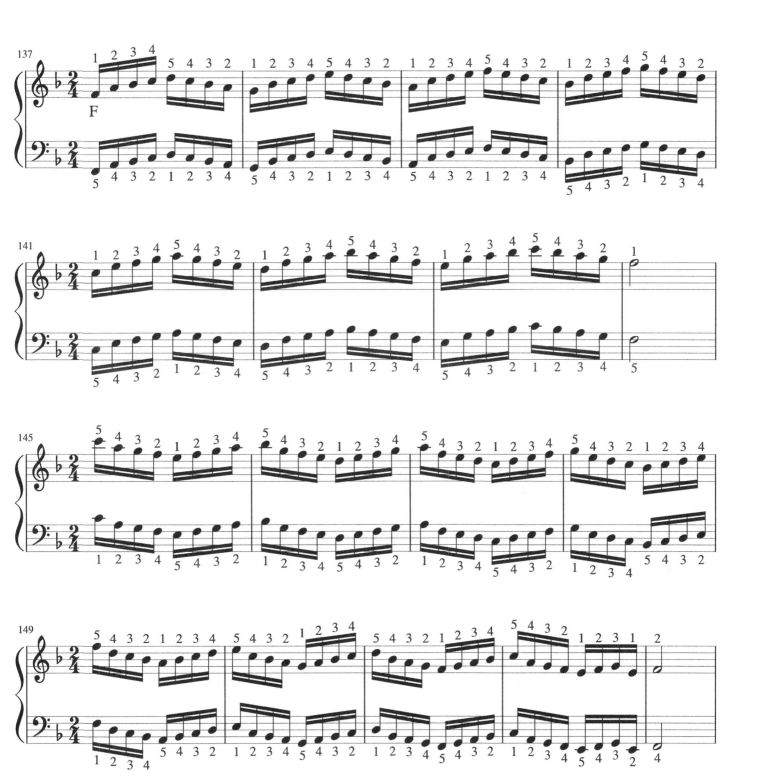

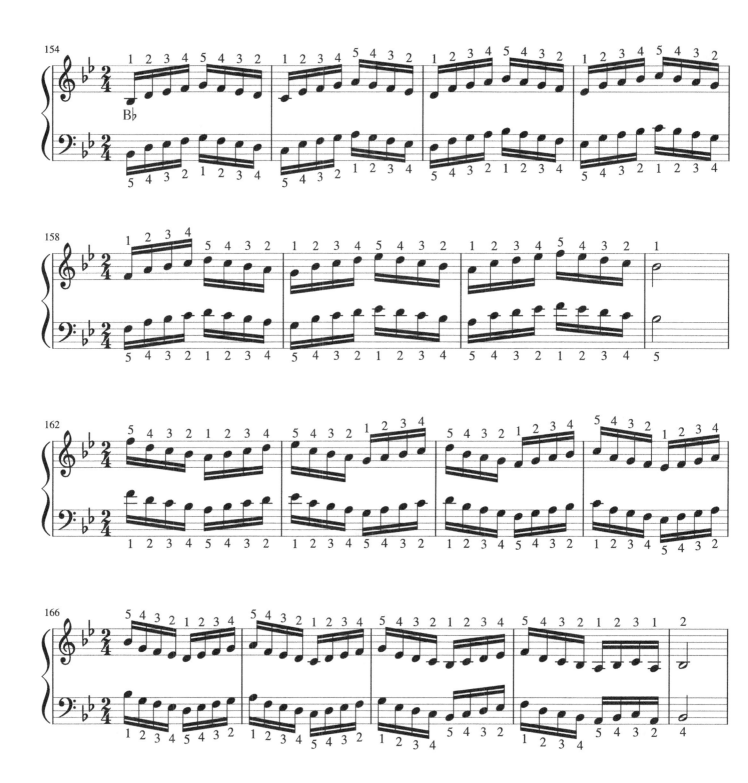

EXERCISES FOR BOTH HANDS IN Ab MAJOR Vol 1

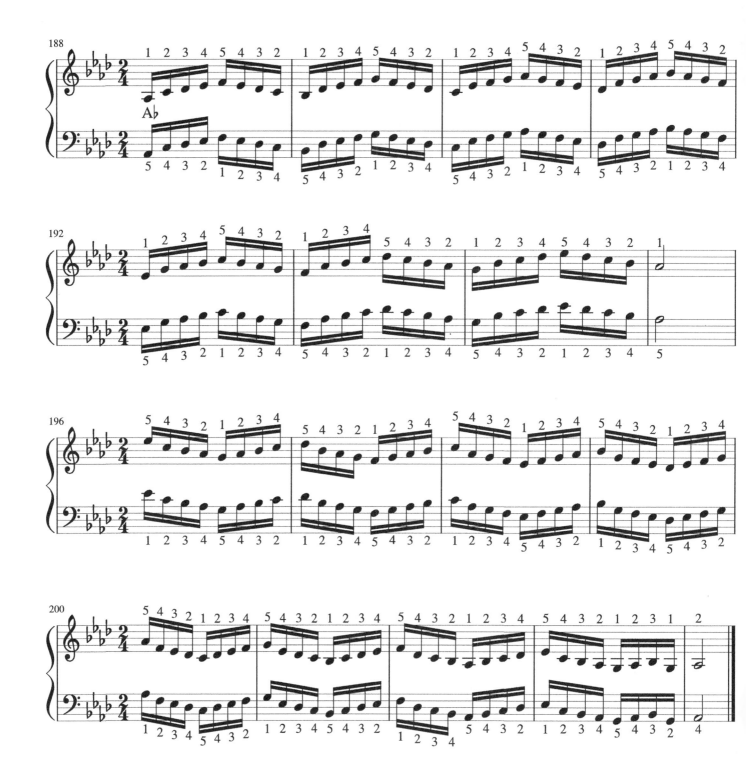

EXERCISES FOR BOTH HANDS IN C MAJOR Vol 2

EXERCISES FOR BOTH HANDS IN D MAJOR Vol 2

EXERCISES FOR BOTH HANDS IN A MAJOR Vol 2

EXERCISES FOR BOTH HANDS IN E MAJOR Vol 2

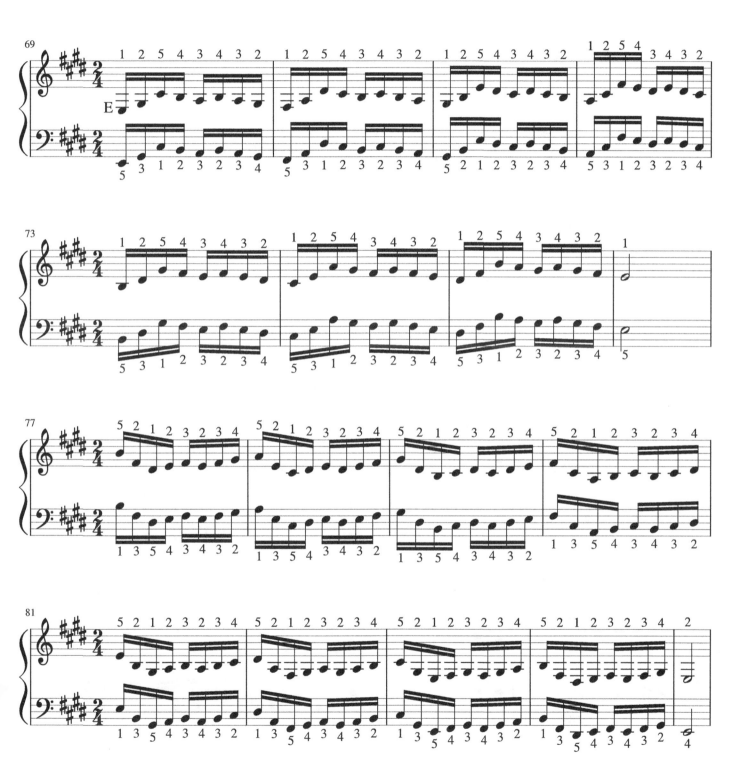

EXERCISES FOR BOTH HANDS IN B MAJOR Vol 2

EXERCISES FOR BOTH HANDS IN F# MAJOR Vol 2

EXERCISES FOR BOTH HANDS IN F MAJOR Vol 2

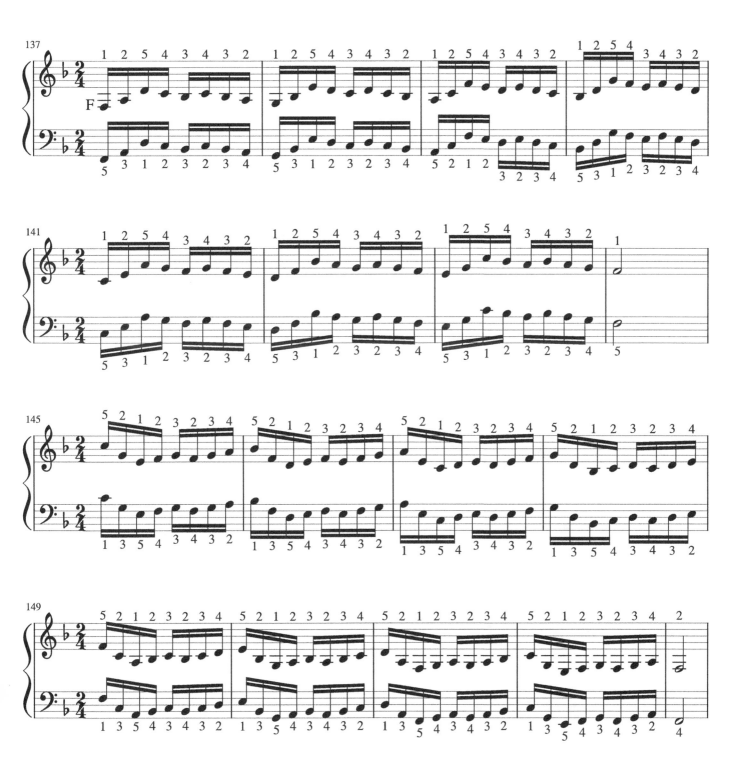

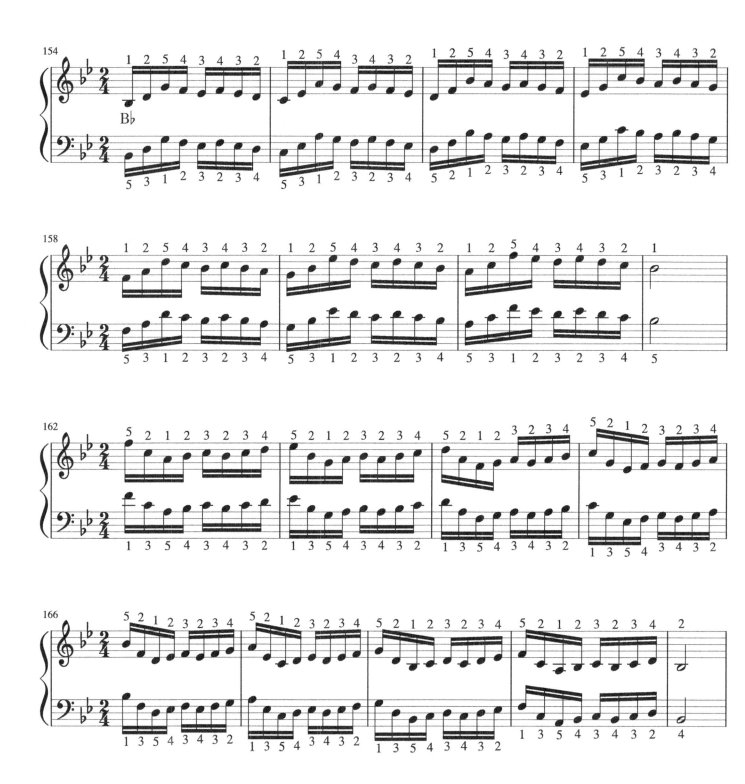

EXERCISES FOR BOTH HANDS IN Eb MAJOR Vol 2

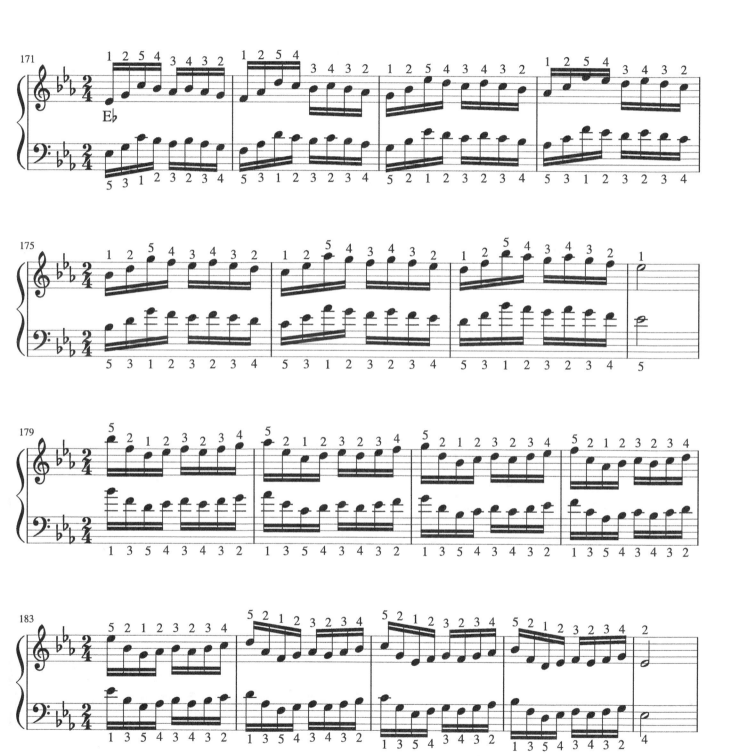

EXERCISES FOR BOTH HANDS IN Ab MAJOR Vol 2

EXERCISES FOR BOTH HANDS IN C MAJOR Vol 3

EXERCISES FOR BOTH HANDS IN G MAJOR Vol 3

EXERCISES FOR BOTH HANDS IN D MAJOR Vol 3

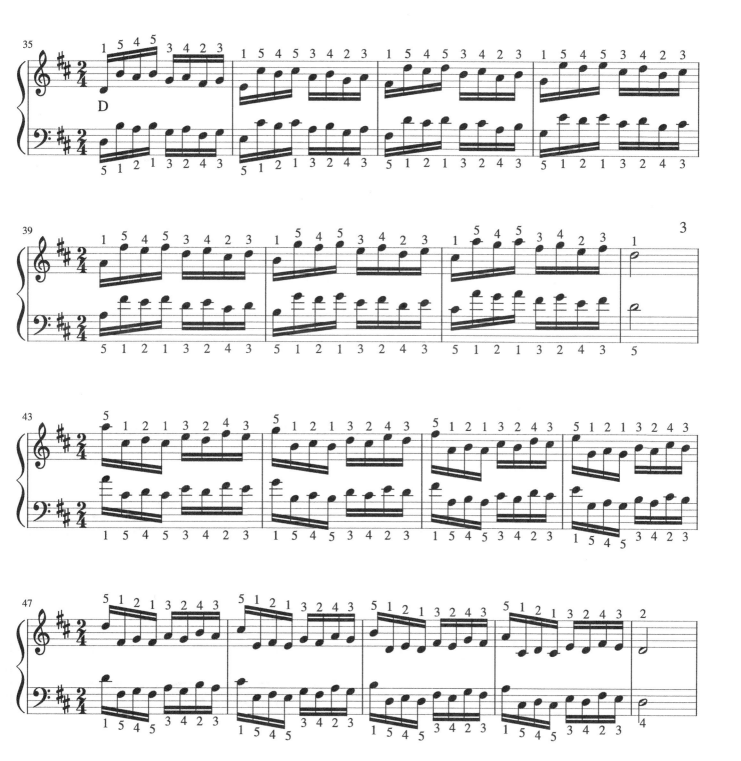

EXERCISES FOR BOTH HANDS IN A MAJOR Vol 3

EXERCISES FOR BOTH HANDS IN E MAJOR Vol 3

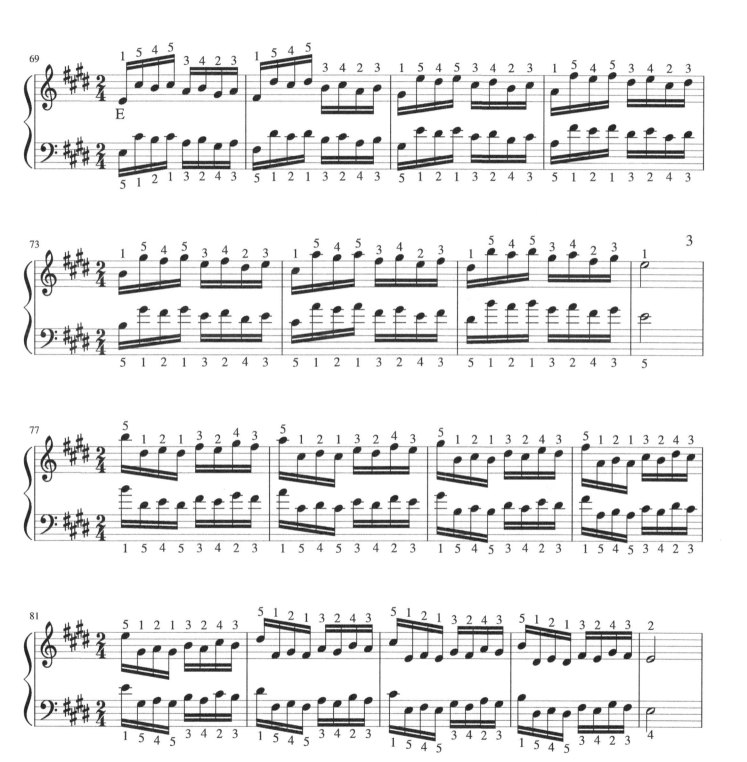

EXERCISES FOR BOTH HANDS IN C# MAJOR Vol 3

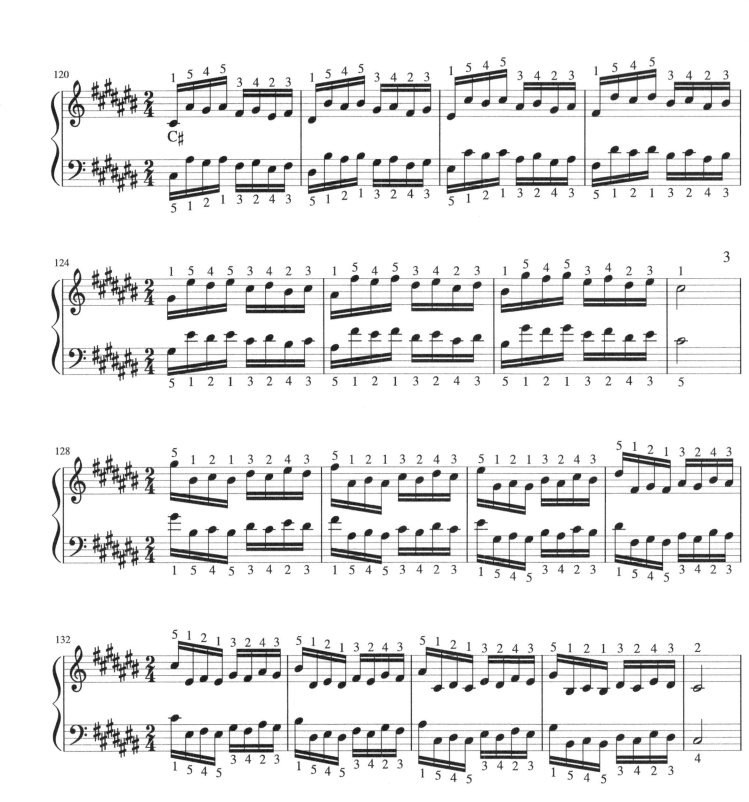

EXERCISES FOR BOTH HANDS IN F MAJOR Vol 3

EXERCISES FOR BOTH HANDS IN C MAJOR Vol 4

EXERCISES FOR BOTH HANDS IN A MAJOR Vol 4

EXERCISES FOR BOTH HANDS IN E MAJOR Vol 4

EXERCISES FOR BOTH HANDS IN B MAJOR Vol 4

EXERCISES FOR BOTH HANDS IN C# MAJOR Vol 4

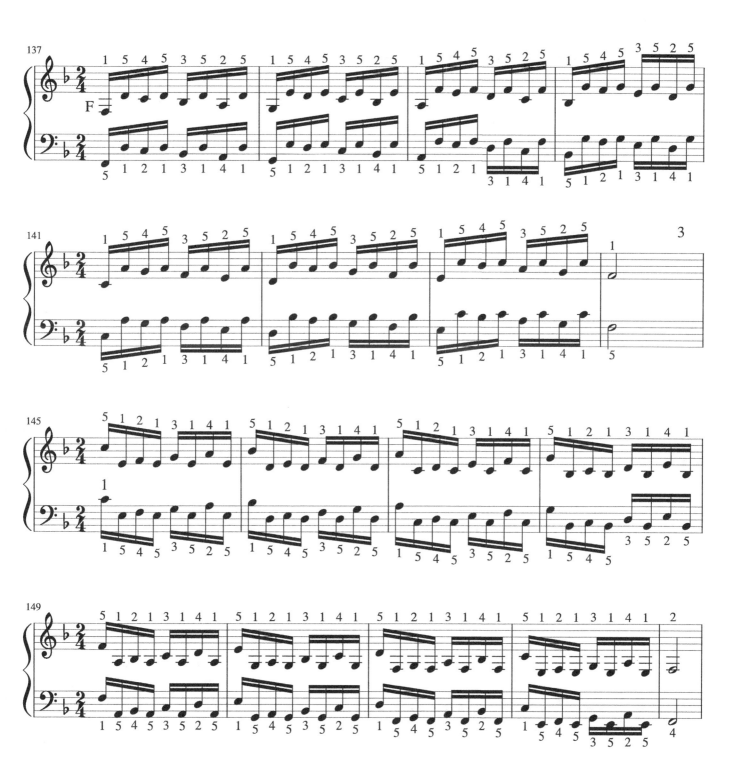

EXERCISES FOR BOTH HANDS IN Bb MAJOR Vol 4

50

EXERCISES FOR BOTH HANDS IN Eb MAJOR Vol 4

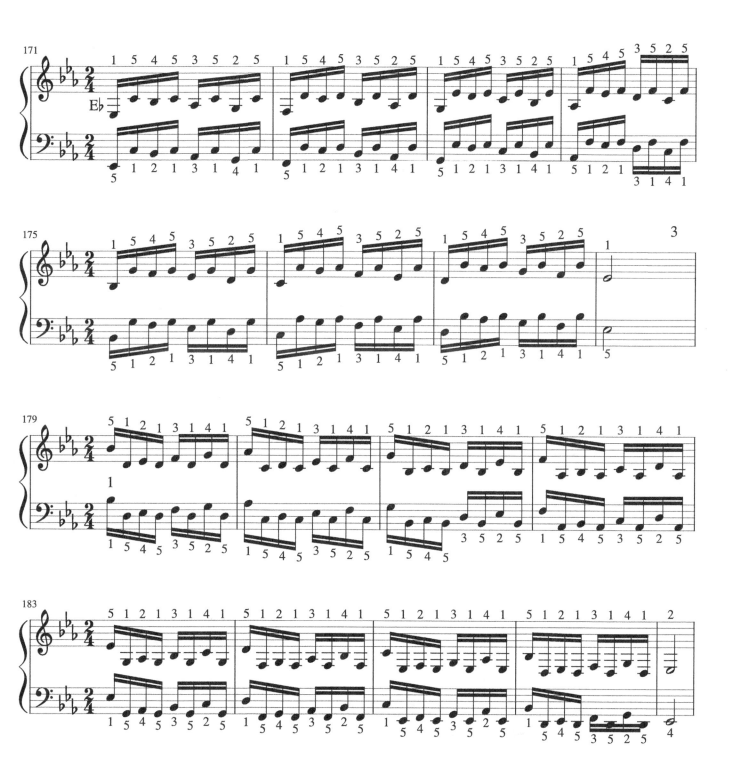

EXERCISES FOR BOTH HANDS IN Ab MAJOR Vol 4

EXERCISES FOR BOTH HANDS IN C MAJOR Vol 5

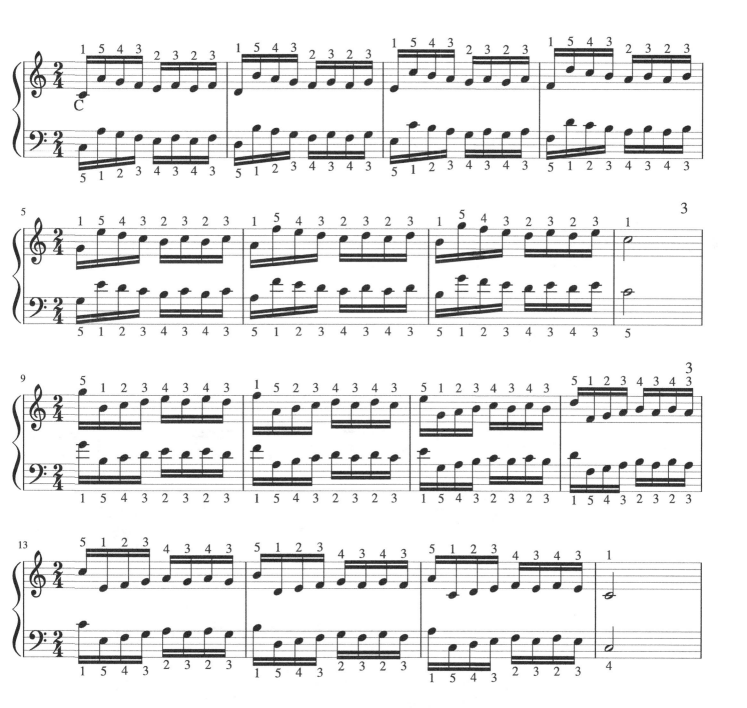

EXERCISES FOR BOTH HANDS IN G MAJOR Vol 5

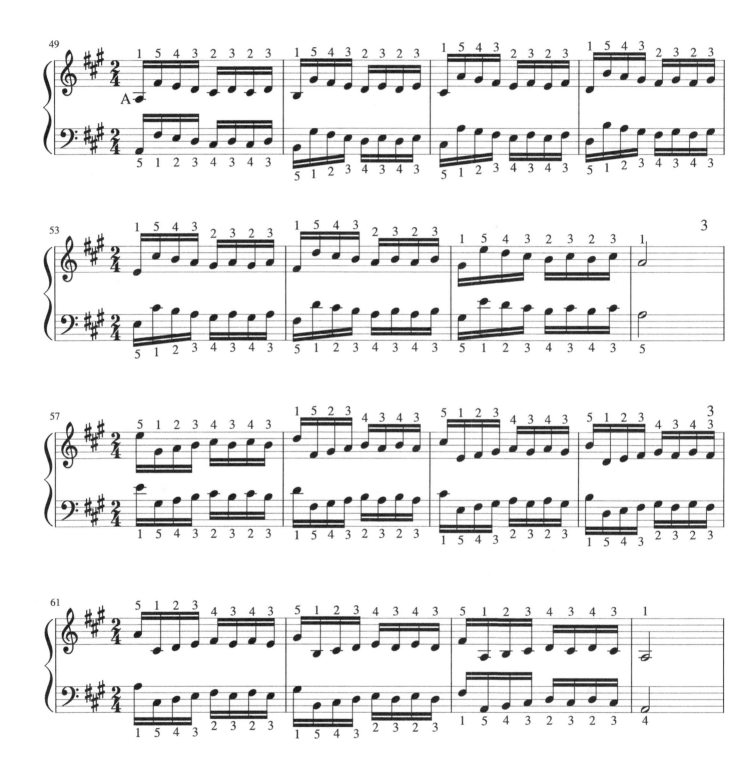

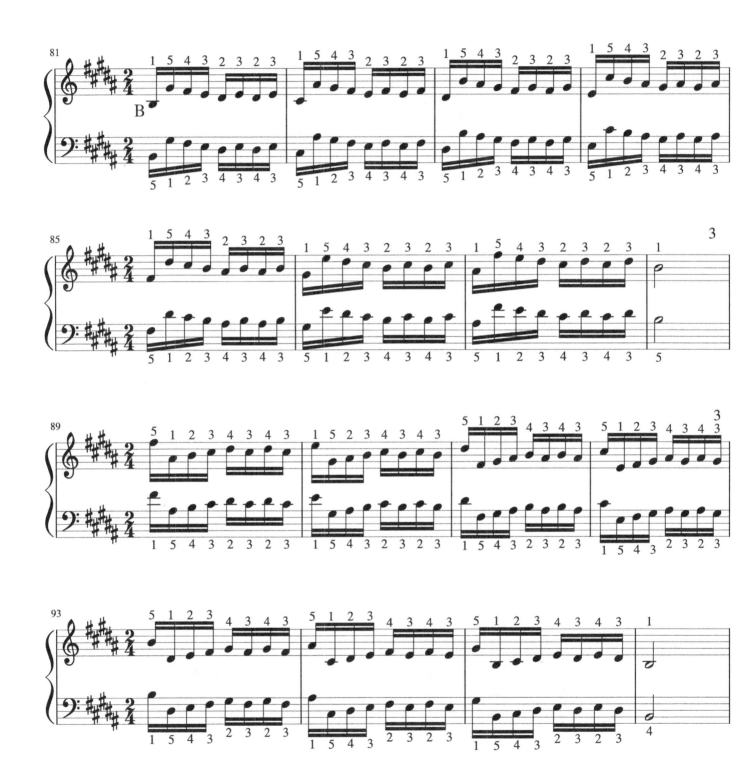

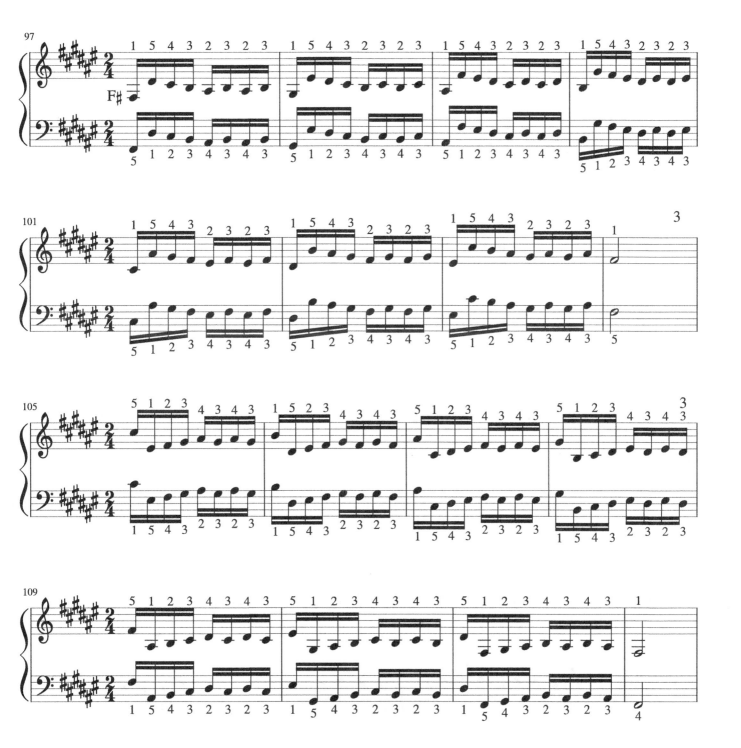

EXERCISES FOR BOTH HANDS IN F MAJOR Vol 5

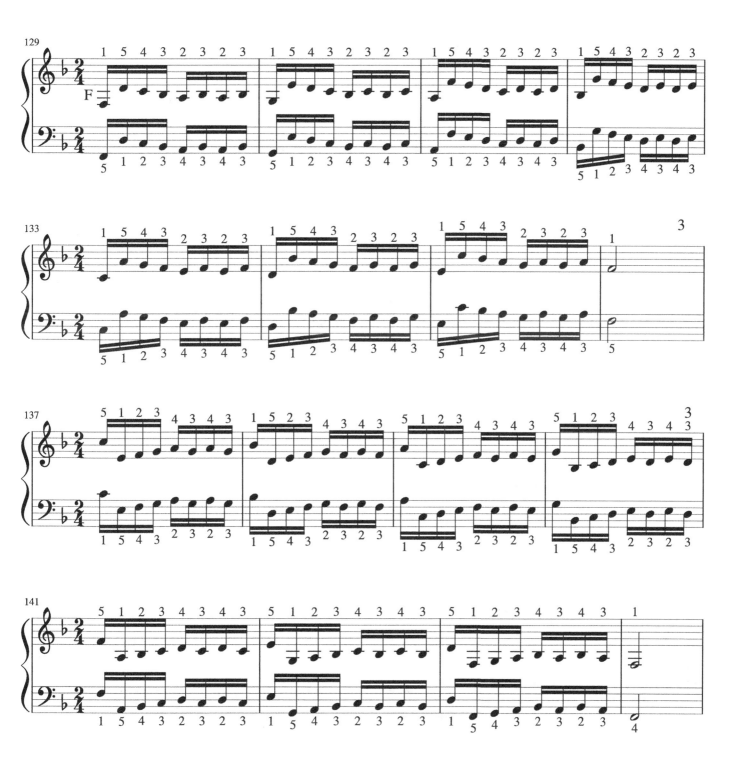

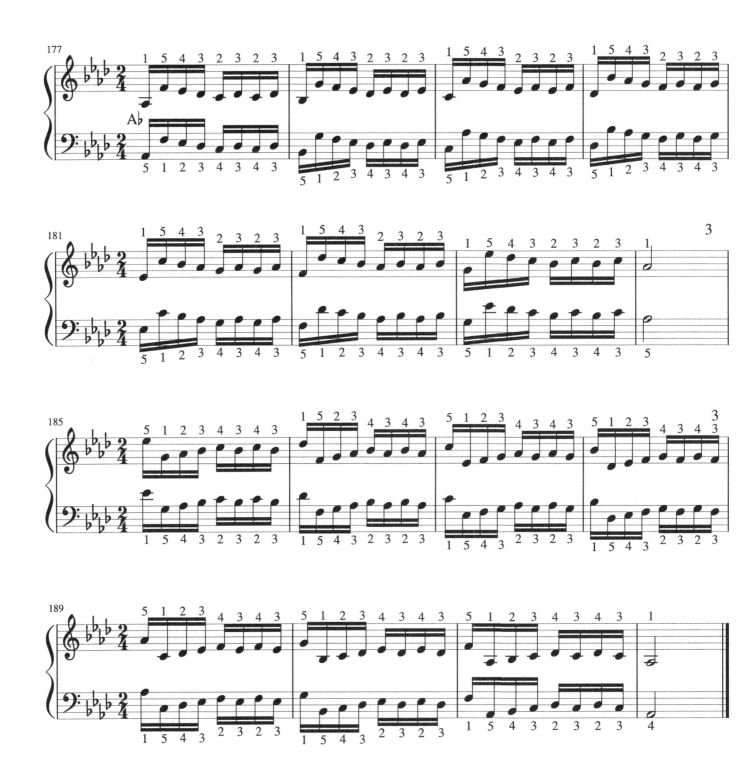

EXERCISES FOR BOTH HANDS IN C MAJOR Vol 6

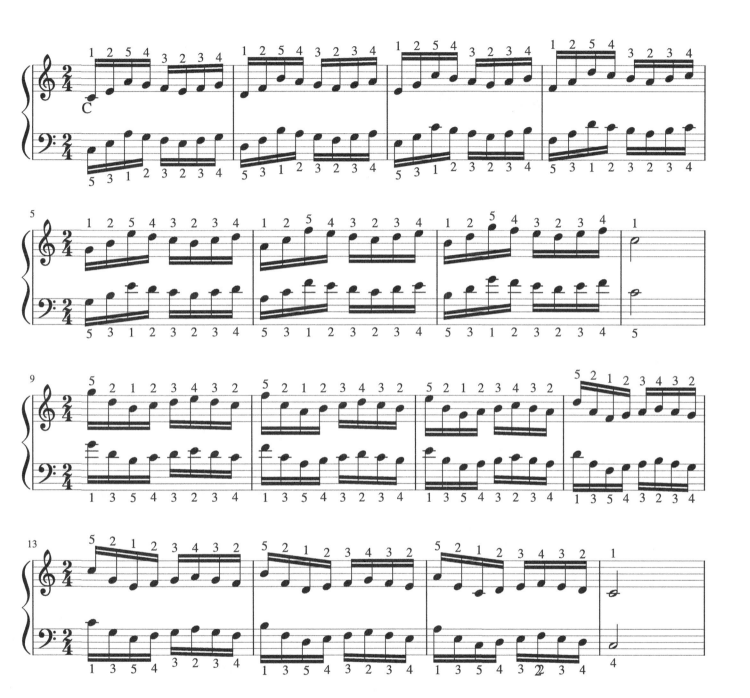

EXERCISES FOR BOTH HANDS IN G MAJOR Vol 6

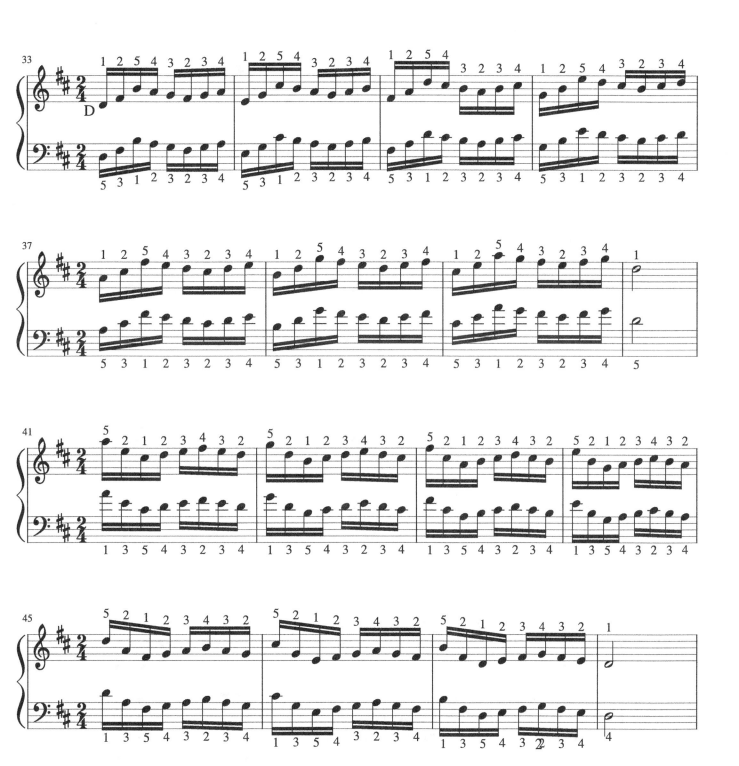

EXERCISES FOR BOTH HANDS IN A MAJOR Vol 6

68

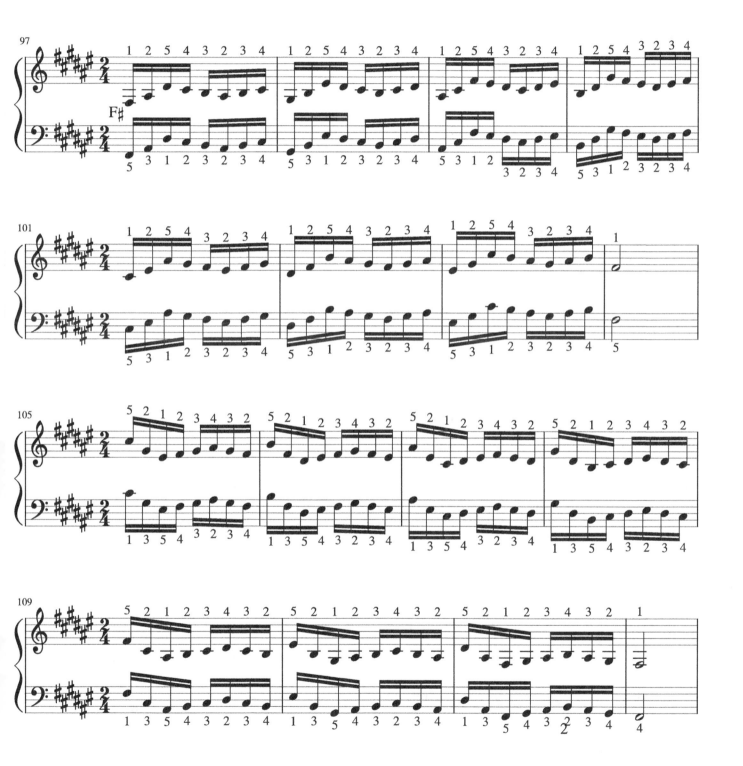

EXERCISES FOR BOTH HANDS IN F MAJOR Vol 6

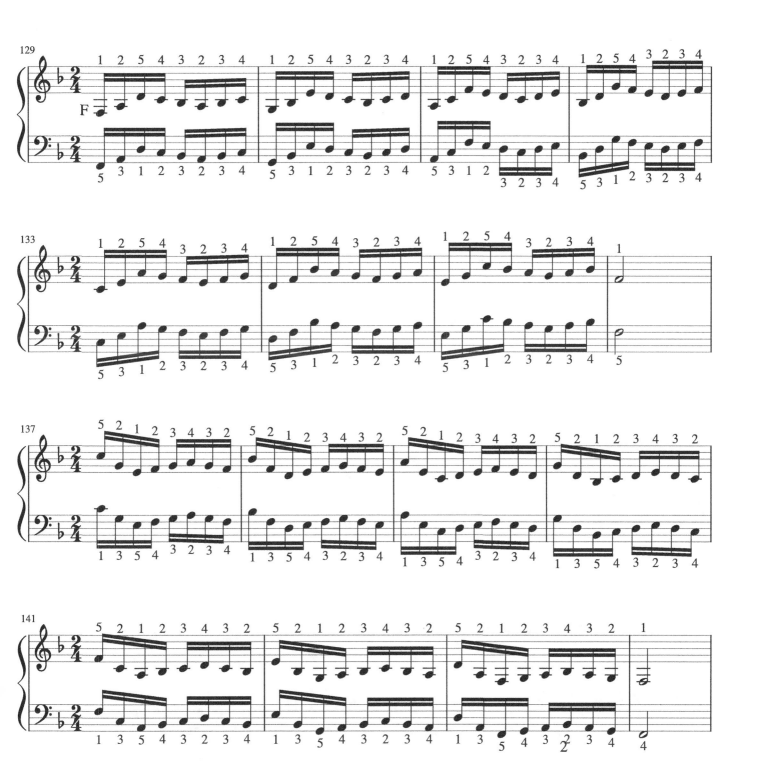

EXERCISES FOR BOTH HANDS IN All KEYS Vol 7
C-Major

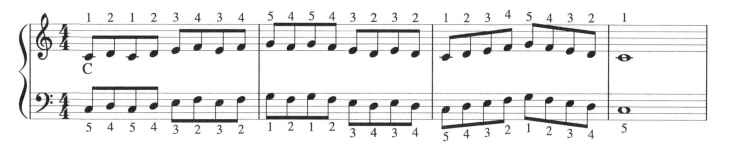

G-Major

D-Major

A-Major

E-Major

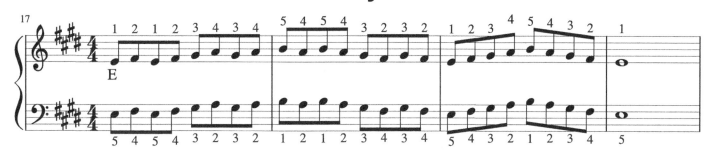

EXERCISES FOR BOTH HANDS IN All KEYS Vol 7
B-Major

F#-Major

C#-Major

F-Major

Bb-Major

Eb-Major

Ab-Major

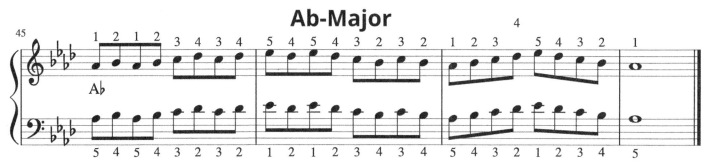

EXERCISES WITH THE CHANGE OF THUMB "TWO FINGERS" VOL 1

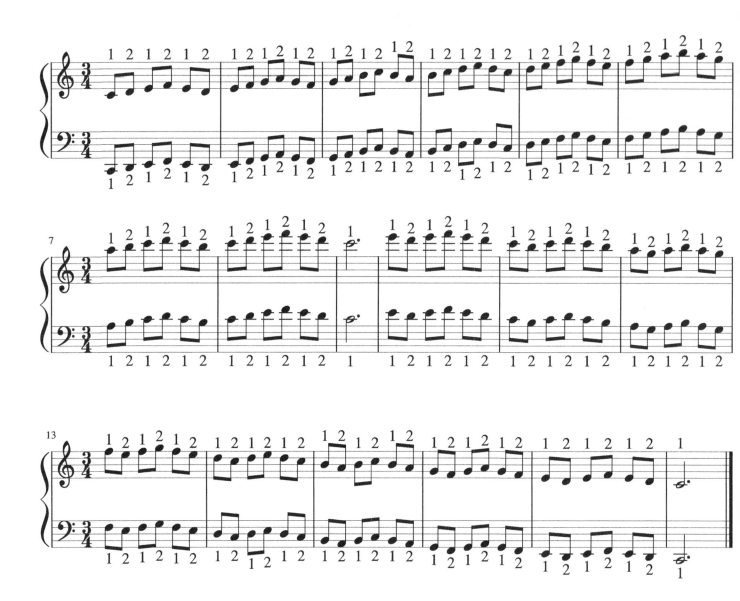

EXERCISES WITH THE CHANGE OF THUMB "THREE FINGERS" VOL 2

EXERCISES WITH THE CHANGE OF THUMB "THREE FINGERS" VOL 2

EXERCISES WITH THE CHANGE OF THUMB "FOUR FINGERS" VOL 3

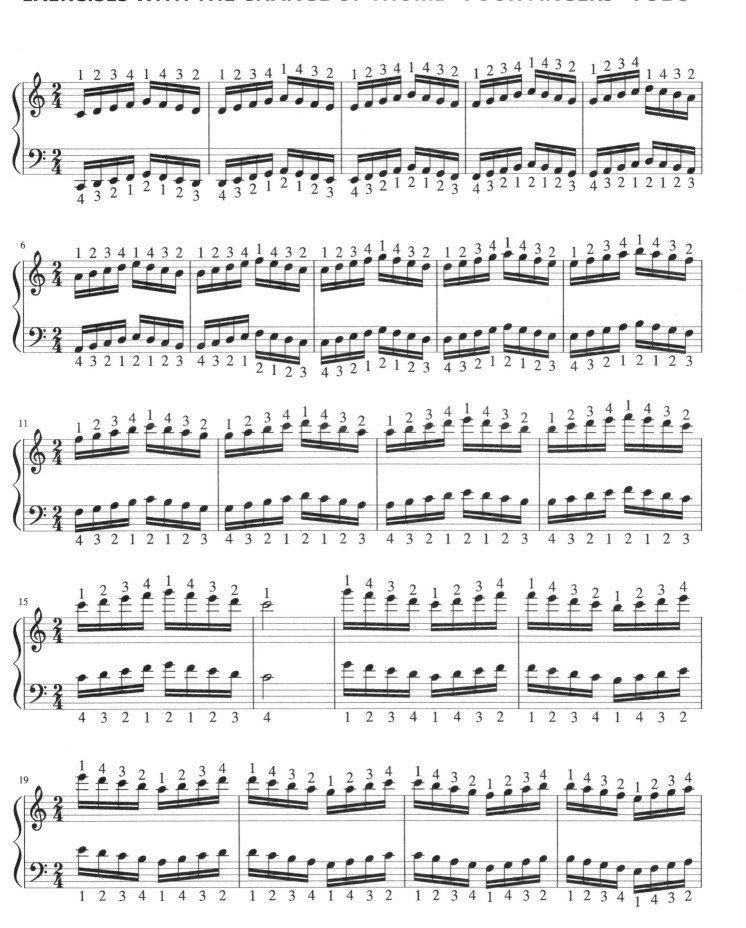

EXERCISES WITH THE CHANGE OF THUMB "FOUR FINGERS" VOL 3

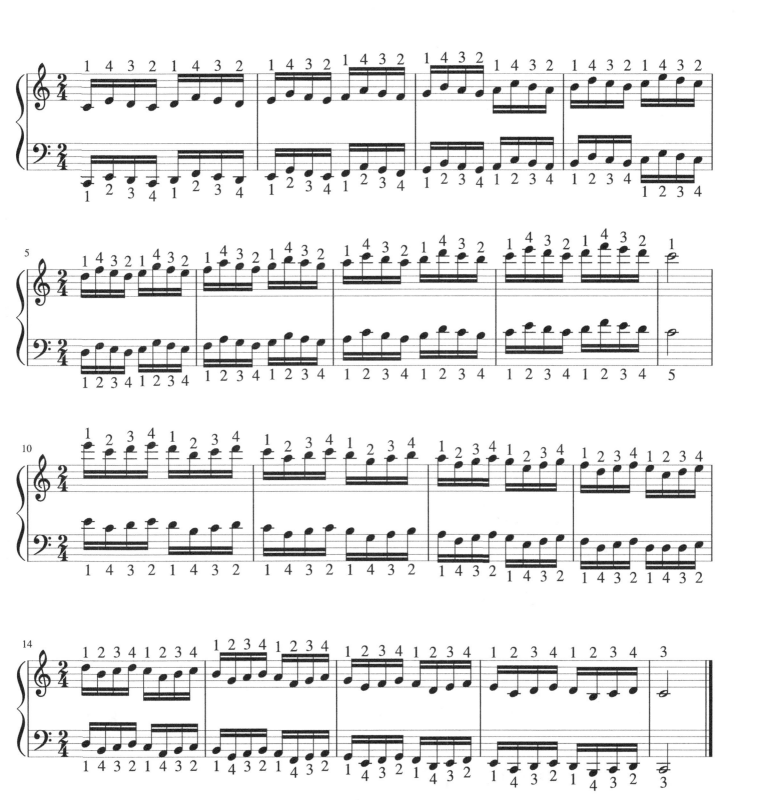

INTRODUCTORY EXERCISES
SCALES - ARPEGGIOS - CHORDS

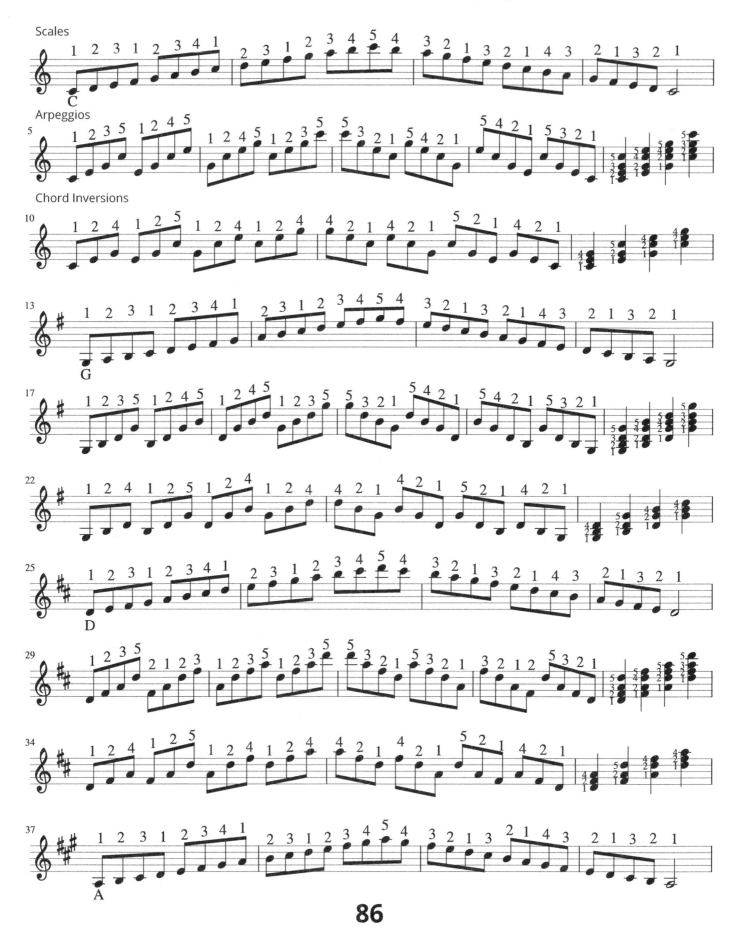

INTRODUCTORY EXERCISES
SCALES - ARPEGGIOS - CHORDS

87

INTRODUCTORY EXERCISES
SCALES - ARPEGGIOS - CHORDS

EXERCISES ON SCALES IN 3 DIFFERENT PATTERNS

EXERCISES ON SCALES IN 3 DIFFERENT PATTERNS

EXERCISES ON SCALES IN 3 DIFFERENT PATTERNS

EXERCISES ON SCALES IN 3 DIFFERENT PATTERNS

EXERCISES ON SCALES IN 3 DIFFERENT PATTERNS

95

EXERCISES ON SCALES IN BOTH HANDS

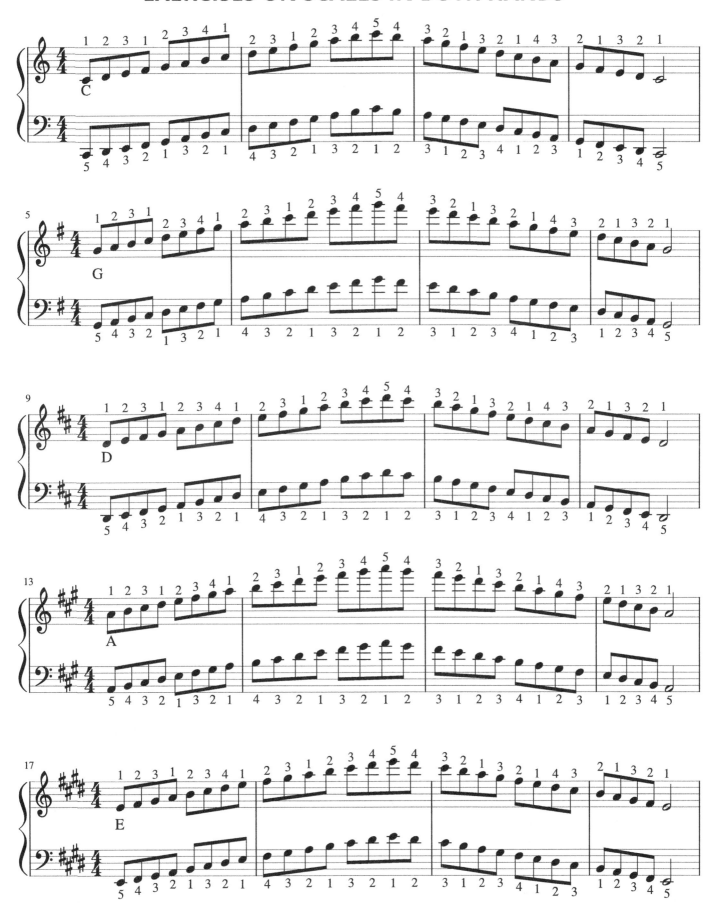

EXERCISES ON SCALES IN BOTH HANDS

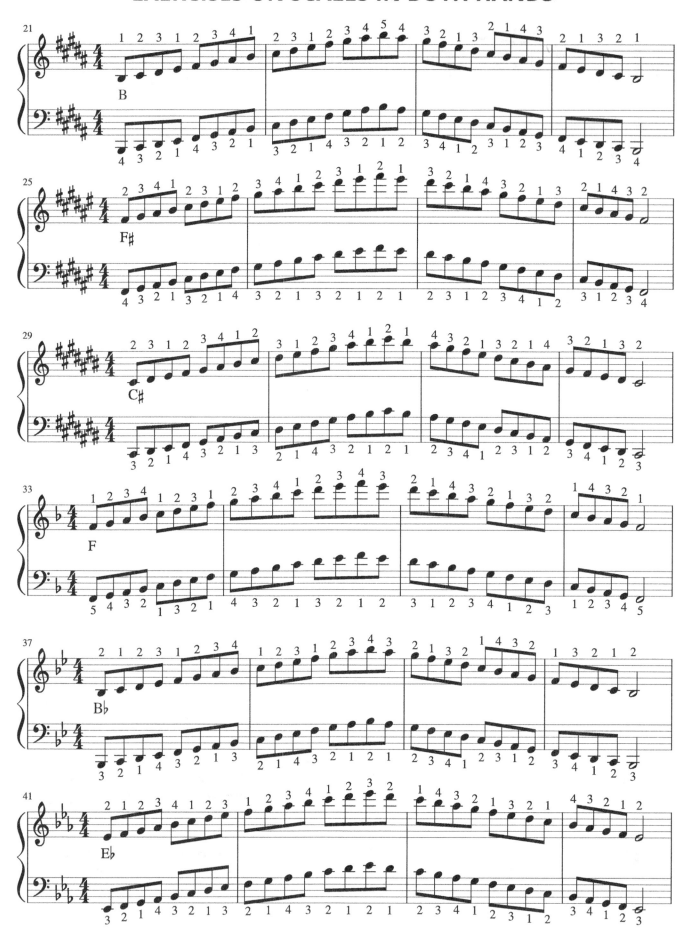

EXERCISES ON SCALES IN BOTH HANDS IN
THE OPPOSITE DIRECTION

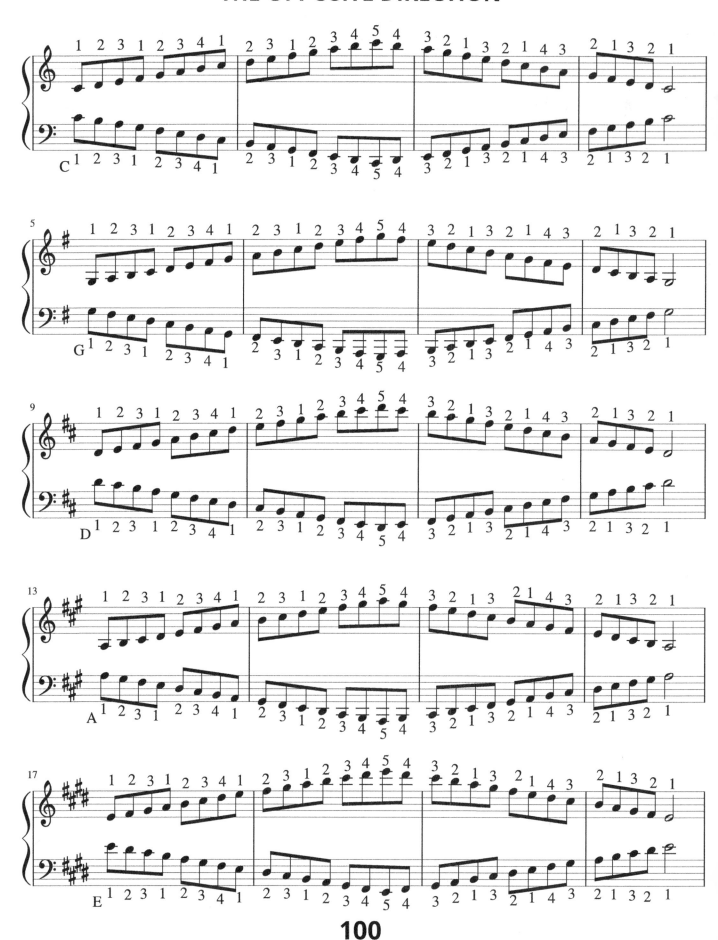

EXERCISES ON SCALES IN BOTH HANDS IN
THE OPPOSITE DIRECTION

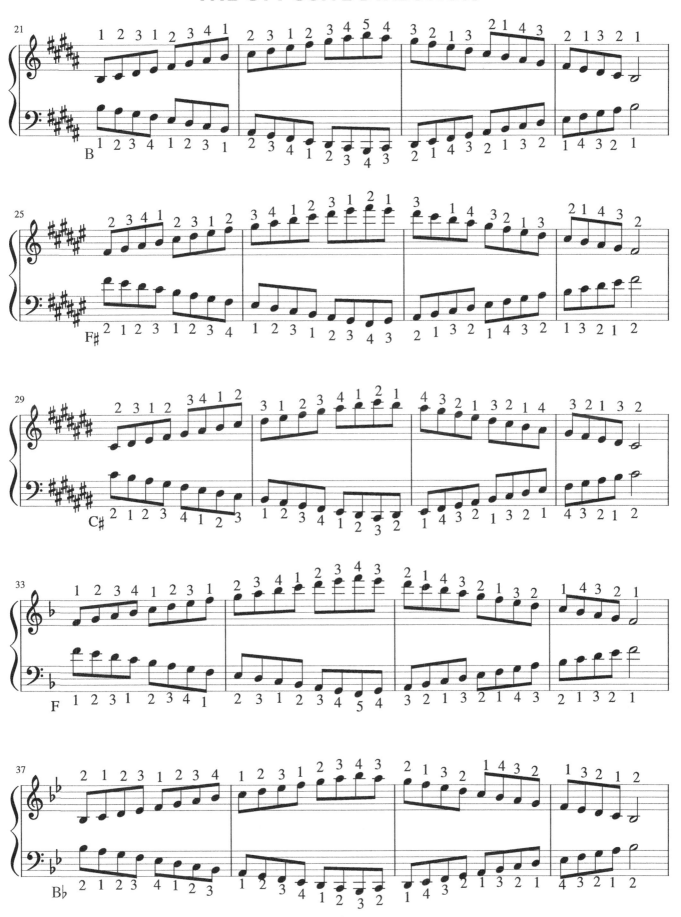

EXERCISES ON SCALES IN BOTH HANDS IN
THE OPPOSITE DIRECTION

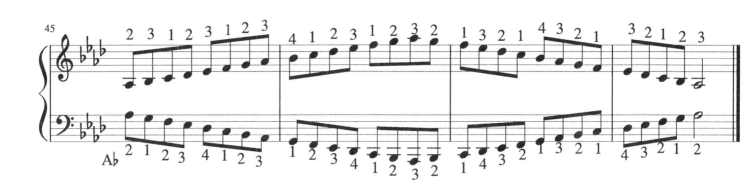

EXERCISES ON CHORDS TOGETHER

EXERCISES ON CHORDS TOGETHER

104

EXERCISES ON CHORDS TOGETHER

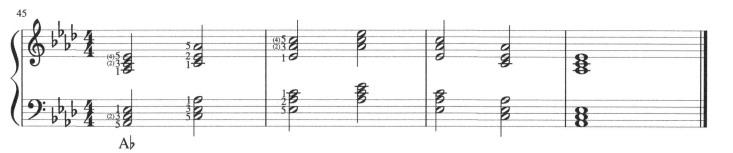

Ab

EXERCISES ON CHORDS FROM THE TOP

EXERCISES ON CHORDS FROM THE TOP

EXERCISES ON CHORDS FROM THE TOP

EXERCISES ON CHORDS IN 3/4 METER

EXERCISES ON CHORDS IN 3/4 METER

EXERCISES ON CHORDS IN 3/4 METER

EXERCISES ON CHORDS IN BOTH HANDS

EXERCISES ON CHORDS IN BOTH HANDS

EXERCISES ON ARPEGGIOS IN DOUBLE

EXERCISES ON ARPEGGIOS IN DOUBLE

EXERCISESON ARPEGGIOS IN DOUBLE

EXERCISES ON ARPEGGIOS IN INTERLACED

EXERCISES ON ARPEGGIOS IN INTERLACED

EXERCISES ON ARPEGGIOS IN INTERLACED

EXERCISES ON ARPEGGIOS IN INTERLACED

EXERCISES ON ARPEGGIOS IN INTERLACED

EXERCISES ON ARPEGGIOS IN TOP-DOWN

EXERCISES ON ARPEGGIOS IN TOP-DOWN

EXERCISES ON ARPEGGIOS IN TOP-DOWN

124

EXERCISES ON ARPEGGIOS IN TOP-DOWN

EXERCISES ON ARPEGGIOS IN BOTH HANDS

EXERCISES ON ARPEGGIOS IN BOTH HANDS

EXERCISES ON ARPEGGIOS FOR BOTH HANDS IN TWO OCTAVES

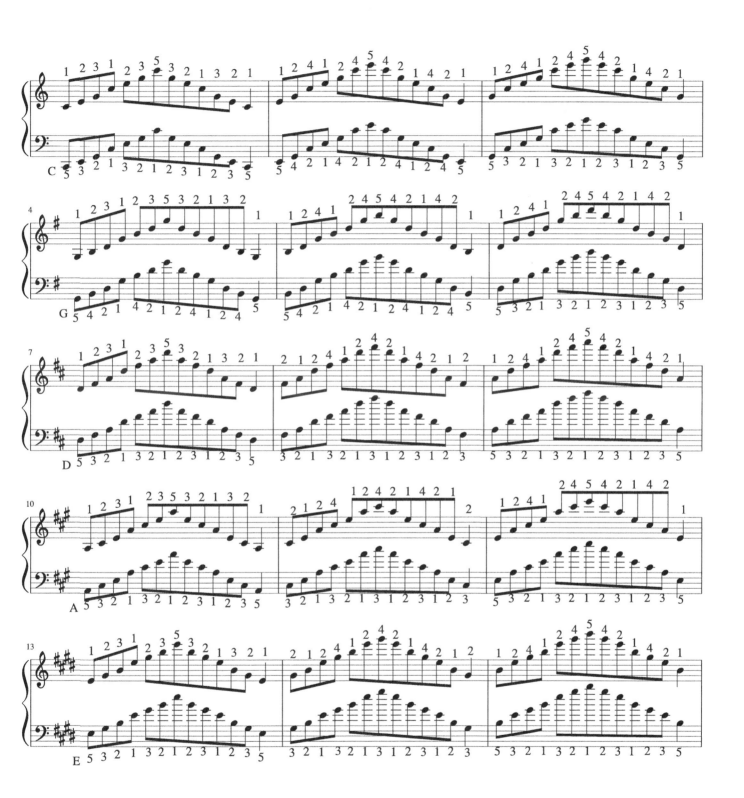

EXERCISES ON ARPEGGIOS FOR BOTH HANDS IN TWO OCTAVES

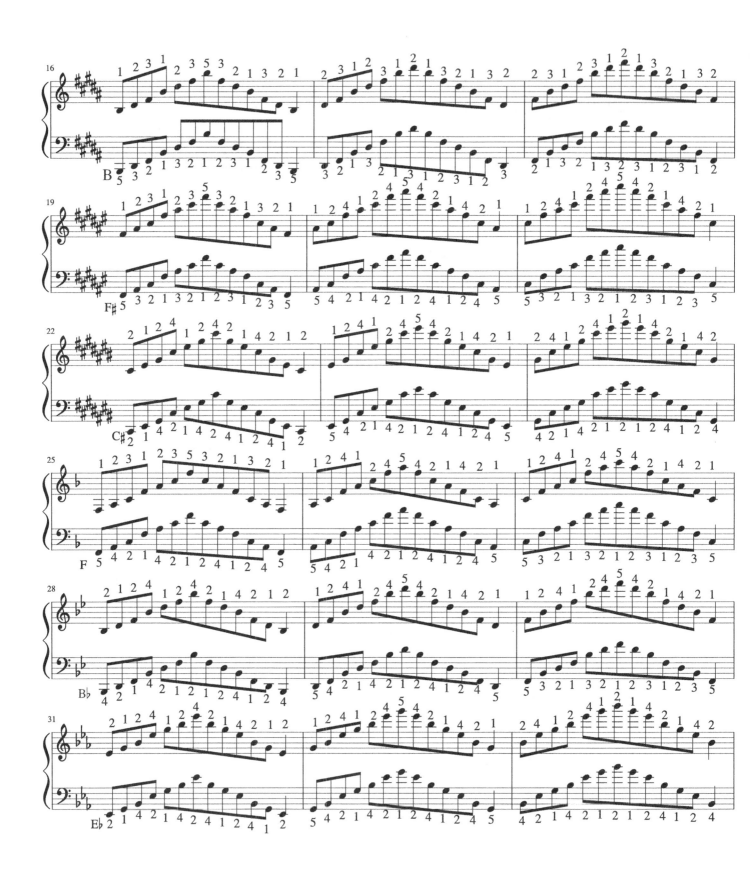

EXERCISES ON ARPEGGIOS FOR BOTH HANDS IN TWO OCTAVES

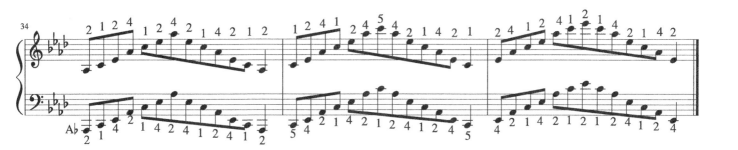

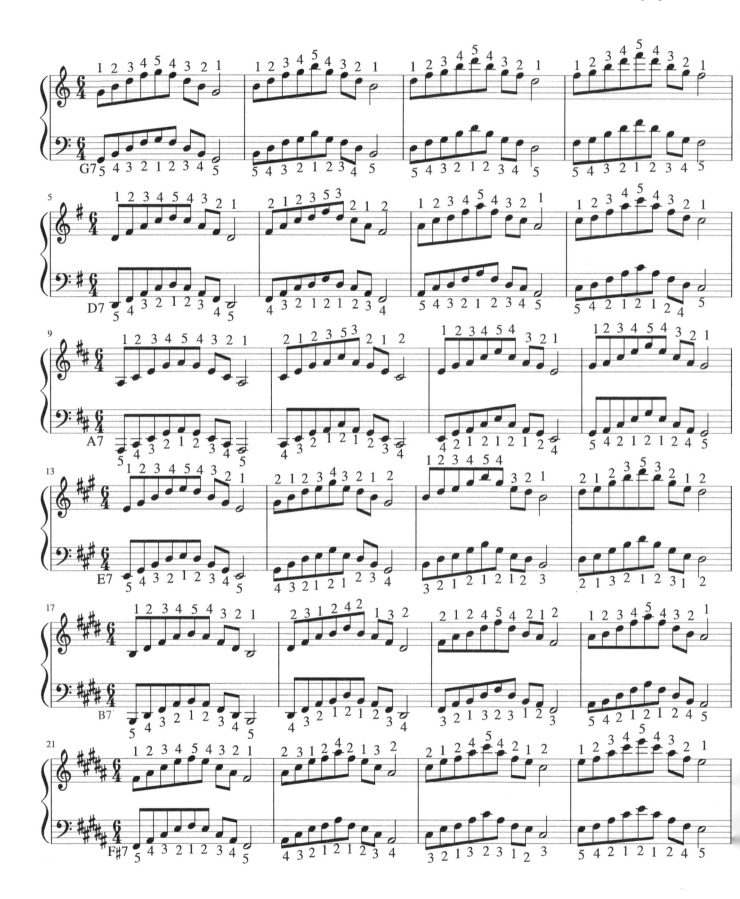

EXERCISES ON ARPEGGIOS DOMINANT SEVENTH (7)

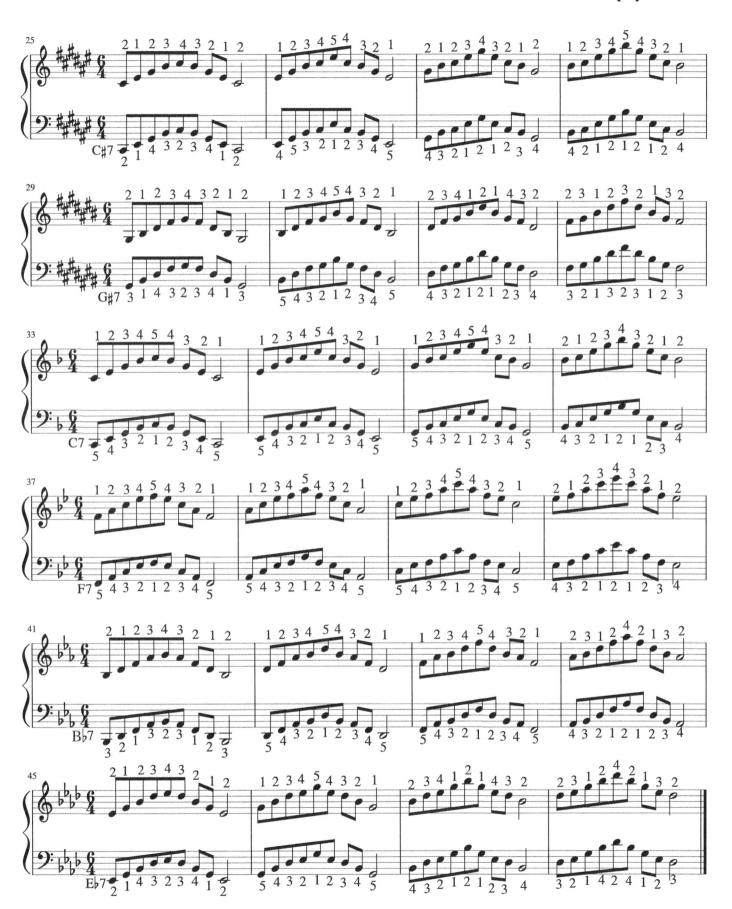

133

See Our Other Books!

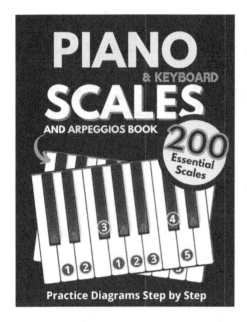

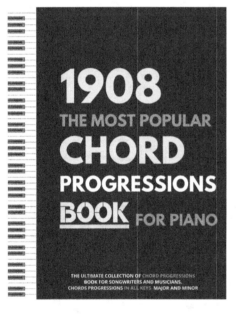

QR Codes To My Books

Summary

In summary, this book delves into the world of practical piano exercises based on scales, chords, and arpeggios. It discusses and shows their exact structure and application in every possible form. It is a valuable resource for musicians wishing to improve their playing technique. If you have reached this point and read the entire book, I would be grateful if you could leave a review. Your opinion is important to me as it helps me to create new and more tailored content to meet the needs of my readers. I would also like to remind you that below are QR codes that will take you to my website and social media pages where you can find more information and resources on music theory.

https://muzycznelekcje.pl/

Thank you very much!

Made in the USA
Las Vegas, NV
04 June 2025

23156777R00077